# COMPLETE SUMMER COOKBOOK 2021

Mirko Lotti

# The benefits of summer seasonal food

You may have heard the term 'eat seasonally' touted by nutrition experts, foodies, and chefs alike. But what does that mean, and what are the benefits to eating seasonal foods? Also, what are the benefits of consuming foods from this season – summer! We'll discuss in this article.

Eating seasonally basically means including foods in your diet that are grown locally at the same time of year that you buy them. These days, due to importing/exporting practices and refrigerated transportation vehicles, we have an abundance of foods available from all over the world. This of course makes it easier to eat many foods, whether they are in season or not. However, there is more to eating seasonally than just a trendy term; there are many benefits to eating foods that are currently being grown and harvested.

# How do you eat healthy?

People often think of healthy eating as dieting. This is not true. Eating healthy is not just about losing weight, it's about feeling better both physically and mentally. Eating healthy is about balance and making sure that your body is getting the necessary nutrients it needs to function properly. Healthy eating habits require that people eat fruits, vegetables, whole grains, fats, proteins, and starches. Keep in mind that healthy eating requires that you're mindful of what you eat and drink, but also how you prepare it. For best results, individuals should avoid fried or processed foods, as well as foods high in added sugars and salts.

## The fundamentals of healthy eating

While some extreme diets may suggest otherwise, we all need a balance of protein, fat, carbohydrates, fiber, vitamins, and minerals in our diets to sustain a healthy body. You don't need to eliminate certain categories of food from your diet, but rather select the healthiest options from each category.

## Top 5 Benefits of Healthy Eating

- Weight loss
- Heart Health
- Strong bones and teeth
- Better mood and energy levels
- Improved memory and brain health

Switching to a healthy diet doesn't have to be an all or nothing proposition. You don't have to be perfect, you don't have to completely eliminate foods you enjoy, and you don't have to change everything all at once—that usually only leads to cheating or giving up on your new eating plan.

To set yourself up for success, try to keep things simple. Eating a healthier diet doesn't have to be complicated.Focus on avoiding packaged and processed foods and opting for more fresh ingredients whenever possible.

- Prepare more of your own meals
- Make the right changes
- Read the labels
- Focus on how you feel after eating
- Drink plenty of water

# Table of Contents

# BOOK 1
# FRESH
# SUMMER
# RECIPES FOR

# BREAKFAST

# EAT COLORFUL
# EAT HEALTHY

# Sweet Potatoes And Apples Mix

**Preparation time:** 10 minutes

**Cooking time**: 1 hour and 10 minutes

**Servings:** 1

**Ingredients:**

- 2 pounds sweet potatoes
- 2 tablespoons water
- ½ pound apples, cored and chopped
- 1 tablespoon low-fat butter

**Directions:**

1. Arrange the potatoes on a lined baking sheet, bake in the oven at 400 degrees F for 1 hour, peel them and mash them in your food processor.
2. Put apples in a pot, add the water, bring to a boil over medium heat, reduce temperature, cook for 10 minutes, transfer to a bowl, add

mashed potatoes, stir well and serve for breakfast.

Enjoy!

**Nutrition:** calories 140, fat 1, fiber 4, carbs 8, protein 6

# Pear Breakfast Salad

**Preparation time:** 10 minutes

**Cooking time:** 0 minutes

**Servings:** 4

**Ingredients:**

- 3 big pears, cored and cut with a spiralizer
- ¾ cup pomegranate seeds
- 5 ounces arugula
- ¾ cup walnuts, roughly chopped

*For the vinaigrette:*

- 2 tablespoons olive oil
- 1 tablespoon coconut sugar
- 1 teaspoon white sesame seeds
- 2 tablespoons apple cider vinegar
- 1 garlic clove, minced
- Black pepper to the taste

## Directions:

1. In a bowl, combine the olive oil with sugar, sesame seeds, vinegar, garlic and pepper and whisk well.
2. In a salad bowl, mix pear with arugula, walnuts and pomegranate seeds, toss, add the vinaigrette, toss and serve for breakfast.

Enjoy!

**Nutrition:** calories 182, fat 2, fiber 7, carbs 11, protein 7

# Breakfast Bulgur Salad

**Preparation time:** 15 minutes

**Cooking time:** 0 minutes

**Servings:** 6

**Ingredients:**

- 1 and ½ cups hot water
- 1 cup bulgur
- Juice of 1 lime
- 4 tablespoons cilantro, chopped
- ½ cup cranberries, dried
- 1 and ½ teaspoons curry powder
- 1/3 cup almonds, sliced
- ¼ cup green onions, chopped
- ½ cup red bell peppers, chopped
- ½ cup carrots, grated
- 4 tablespoons pepitas
- 1 tablespoon olive oil
- Black pepper to the taste

**Directions:**

1. Put bulgur into a bowl, add boiling water, cover, leave aside for 15 minutes, fluff bulgur with a fork and transfer to a salad bowl.
2. Add lime juice, cilantro, cranberries, almonds, bell peppers, onions, carrots, curry powder, pepitas, black pepper and the oil, toss and serve for breakfast.

Enjoy!

**Nutrition:** calories 190, fat 3, fiber 3, carbs 13, protein 10

# Black Bean Breakfast Salad

**Preparation time:** 15 minutes

**Cooking time:** 0 minutes

**Servings:** 4

**Ingredients:**

- 1 and ½ cups canned black beans, no-salt-added, drained and rinsed
- ½ teaspoon garlic powder
- ½ teaspoon smoked paprika
- 2 teaspoons chili powder
- Black pepper to the taste
- 1 teaspoon cumin, ground
- 1 and ½ cups canned chickpeas, no-salt-added, drained and rinsed
- ¼ teaspoon cinnamon powder
- 1 lettuce head, chopped
- 1 red bell pepper, chopped
- 2 tomatoes, chopped

- 1 avocado, pitted, peeled and chopped
- 1 cup corn kernels, chopped

*For the salad dressing:*

- 2 tablespoons lemon juice
- ¾ cup cashews, soaked and drained
- ½ cup water
- 1 garlic clove, minced
- 1 tablespoon apple cider vinegar
- ½ teaspoon onion powder
- 1 teaspoon chives, chopped
- ½ teaspoon oregano, dried
- 1 teaspoon dill, dried
- 1 teaspoon cumin, ground
- ½ teaspoon smoked paprika

## Directions:

1. In your blender, mix cashews with water, 2 tablespoons lemon juice, 1 tablespoon vinegar, 1 garlic clove, ½ teaspoon onion powder, dill, oregano, chives, cumin and ½ teaspoon paprika, blend really well and leave aside for now.

2. In a salad bowl, mix black beans with chili powder, ½ teaspoon garlic powder, ½ teaspoon paprika, chickpeas, cinnamon and black pepper to the taste and stir really well.

3. Add lettuce leaves, tomatoes, corn, avocado and bell peppers, toss everything, drizzle the salad dressing, mix everything again and serve for breakfast.

**Nutrition:** calories 190, fat 4, fiber 10, carbs 11, protein 11

# Chickpeas Breakfast Salad

**Preparation time:** 10 minutes

**Cooking time:** 0 minutes

**Servings:** 2

**Ingredients:**

- 16 ounces canned chickpeas, no-salt-added, drained and rinsed
- 1 handful baby spinach leaves
- ½ tablespoon lemon juice
- 4 tablespoons olive oil
- 1 teaspoon cumin, ground
- Black pepper to the taste
- ½ teaspoon chili flakes

**Directions:**

1. In a bowl, mix lemon juice, oil, cumin, black pepper and chili flakes and whisk well.

2.  In a salad bowl, mix chickpeas with spinach, add salad dressing, toss to coat and serve for breakfast.

Enjoy!

**Nutrition:** calories 220, fat 3, fiber 6, carbs 12, protein 8

# Mediterranean Breakfast Salad

**Preparation time:** 10 minutes

**Cooking time:** 0 minutes

**Servings:** 4

**Ingredients:**

- 1 handful kalamata olives, pitted and sliced
- 1-pint cherry tomatoes, halved
- 4 tomatoes, chopped
- 1 and ½ cucumbers, sliced
- 1 red onion, chopped
- 2 tablespoons oregano, chopped
- 1 tablespoon mint, chopped

*For the salad dressing:*

- 1 teaspoon coconut sugar
- 2 tablespoons balsamic vinegar
- ¼ cup olive oil
- 1 garlic clove, minced

- 2 teaspoons Italian herbs, dried
- Black pepper to the taste

**Directions:**

1. In a salad bowl, mix cherry tomatoes with tomatoes, olives, cucumbers, onion, mint and oregano and toss
2. In another bowl, mix sugar with vinegar, oil, garlic, dried Italian herbs and black pepper, whisk well, add to your salad, toss to coat and serve for breakfast.

Enjoy!

**Nutrition:** calories 180, fat 2, fiber 3, carbs 6, protein 9

# Easy Veggie Muffins

**Preparation time:** 10 minutes

**Cooking time:** 40 minutes

**Servings:** 4

**Ingredients:**

- ¾ cup cheddar cheese, shredded
- 1 cup green onion, chopped
- 1 cup tomatoes, chopped
- 1 cup broccoli, chopped
- 2 cups non-fat milk
- 1 cup biscuit ix
- 4 eggs
- Cooking spray
- 1 teaspoon Italian seasoning
- A pinch of black pepper

**Directions:**

1. Grease a muffin tray with cooking spray and divide broccoli, tomatoes cheese and onions in each muffin cup.
2. In a bowl, combine green onions with milk, biscuit mix, eggs, pepper and Italian seasoning, whisk well and pour into the muffin tray as well.
3. Cook the muffins in the oven at 375 degrees F for 40 minutes, divide them between plates and serve.

Enjoy!

**Nutrition:** calories 212, fat 2, fiber 3, carbs 12, protein 6

# Carrot Muffins

**Preparation time:** 10 minutes

**Cooking time:** 30 minutes

**Servings:** 5

**Ingredients:**

- 1 and ½ cups whole wheat flour
- ½ cup stevia
- 1 teaspoon baking powder
- ½ teaspoon cinnamon powder
- ½ teaspoon baking soda
- ¼ cup natural apple juice
- ¼ cup olive oil
- 1 egg
- 1 cup fresh cranberries
- 2 carrots, grated
- 2 teaspoons ginger, grated
- ¼ cup pecans, chopped
- Cooking spray

**Directions:**

1. In a large bowl, combine the flour with the stevia, baking powder, cinnamon and baking soda and stir well.
2. Add apple juice, oil, egg, cranberries, carrots, ginger and pecans and stir really well.
3. Grease a muffin tray with cooking spray, divide the muffin mix, introduce in the oven and cook at 375 degrees F for 30 minutes.
4. Divide the muffins between plates and serve for breakfast.

Enjoy!

**Nutrition:** calories 212, fat 3, fiber 6, carbs 14, protein 6

# Pineapple Oatmeal

**Preparation time:** 10 minutes

**Cooking time:** 25 minutes

**Servings:** 4

## Ingredients:

- 2 cups old-fashioned oats
- 1 cup walnuts, chopped
- 2 cups pineapple, cubed
- 1 tablespoon ginger, grated
- 2 cups non-fat milk
- 2 eggs
- 2 tablespoons stevia
- 2 teaspoons vanilla extract

## Directions:

1. In a bowl, combine the oats with the pineapple, walnuts and ginger, stir and divide into 4 ramekins.

2. In a bowl, combine the milk with the eggs, stevia and vanilla, whisk well and pour over the oats mix.
3. Introduce in the oven and cook at 400 degrees F for 25 minutes.
4. Serve for breakfast.

Enjoy!

**Nutrition:** calories 211, fat 2, fiber 4, carbs 14, protein 6

# Spinach Muffins

**Preparation time:** 10 minutes

**Cooking time:** 30 minutes

**Servings:** 6

**Ingredients:**

- 6 eggs
- ½ cup non-fat milk
- 1 cup low-fat cheese, crumbled
- 4 ounces spinach
- ½ cup roasted red pepper, chopped
- 2 ounces prosciutto, chopped
- Cooking spray

**Directions:**

1. In a bowl, combine the eggs with the milk, cheese, spinach, red pepper and prosciutto and whisk well.

2. Grease a muffin tray with cooking spray, divide the muffin mix, introduce in the oven and bake at 350 degrees F for 30 minutes.

3. Divide between plates and serve for breakfast. Enjoy!

**Nutrition:** calories 155, fat 10, fiber 1, carbs 4, protein 10

# Chia Seeds Breakfast Mix

**Preparation time:** 8 hours
**Cooking time:** 0 minutes
**Servings:** 4

## Ingredients:

- 2 cups old-fashioned oats
- 4 tablespoons chia seeds
- 4 tablespoons coconut sugar
- 3 cups coconut milk
- 1 teaspoon lemon zest, grated
- 1 cup blueberries

## Directions:

1. In a bowl, combine the oats with chia seeds, sugar, milk, lemon zest and blueberries, stir, divide into cups and keep in the fridge for 8 hours.
2. Serve for breakfast.

Enjoy!

**Nutrition:** calories 283, fat 12, fiber 3, carbs 13, protein 8

# Breakfast Fruits Bowls

**Preparation time:** 10 minutes

**Cooking time:** 0 minutes

**Servings:** 2

**Ingredients:**

- 1 cup mango, chopped
- 1 banana, sliced
- 1 cup pineapple, chopped
- 1 cup almond milk

**Directions:**

1. In a bowl, combine the mango with the banana, pineapple and almond milk, stir, divide into smaller bowls and serve for breakfast.

Enjoy!

**Nutrition:** calories 182, fat 2, fiber 4, carbs 12, protein 6

# Pumpkin Breakfast Cookies

**Preparation time:** 10 minutes

**Cooking time:** 25 minutes

**Servings:** 6

**Ingredients:**

- 2 cups whole wheat flour
- 1 cup old-fashioned oats
- 1 teaspoon baking soda
- 1 teaspoon pumpkin pie spice
- 15 ounces pumpkin puree
- 1 cup coconut oil, melted
- 1 cup coconut sugar
- 1 egg
- ½ cup pepitas, roasted
- ½ cup cherries, dried

## Directions:

1.  In a bowl, combine the flour with the oats, baking soda, pumpkin spice, pumpkin puree, oil, sugar, egg, pepitas and cherries, stir well, shape medium cookies out of this mix, arrange them all on a lined baking sheet, introduce in the oven and bake at 350 degrees F for 25 minutes.
2.  Serve the cookies for breakfast.

Enjoy!

**Nutrition:** calories 281, fat 12, fiber 3, carbs 14, protein 6

# Veggie Scramble

**Preparation time:** 10 minutes
**Cooking time:** 2 minutes
**Servings:** 1

**Ingredients:**

- 1 egg
- 1 tablespoon water
- ¼ cup broccoli, chopped
- ¼ cup mushrooms, chopped
- A pinch of black pepper
- 1 tablespoon low-fat mozzarella, shredded
- 1 tablespoon walnuts, chopped
- Cooking spray

**Directions:**

1. Grease a ramekin with cooking spray, add the egg, water, pepper, mushrooms and broccoli and whisk well.

2. Introduce in the microwave and cook for 2 minutes.
3. Add mozzarella and walnuts on top and serve for breakfast.

Enjoy!

**Nutrition:** calories 211, fat 2, fiber 4, carbs 12, protein 6

# Mushrooms and Turkey Breakfast

**Preparation time:** 10 minutes

**Cooking time:** 1 hour and 5 minutes

**Servings:** 12

**Ingredients:**

- 8 ounces whole wheat bread, cubed
- 12 ounces turkey sausage, chopped
- 2 cups fat-free milk
- 5 ounces low-fat cheddar, shredded
- 3 eggs
- ½ cup green onions, chopped
- 1 cup mushrooms, chopped
- ½ teaspoon sweet paprika
- A pinch of black pepper
- 2 tablespoons low-fat parmesan, grated

## Directions:

1. Spread bread cubes on a lined baking sheet, introduce in the oven and bake at 400 degrees F for 8 minutes.
2. Meanwhile, heat up a pan over medium-high heat, add turkey sausage, stir and brown for 7 minutes.
3. In a bowl, combine the milk with the cheddar, eggs, parmesan, black pepper and paprika and whisk well.
4. Add mushrooms, sausage, bread cubes and green onions, stir, pour into a baking dish, introduce in the oven and bake at 350 degrees F for 50 minutes.
5. Slice, divide between plates and serve for breakfast.

Enjoy!

**Nutrition:** calories 221, fat 3, fiber 6, carbs 12, protein 6

# Delicious Omelet

**Preparation time:** 10 minutes

**Cooking time:** 6 minutes

**Servings:** 2

**Ingredients:**

- 2 eggs
- 2 tablespoons water
- 1 teaspoon olive oil
- ¼ cup low-fat Mexican cheese, shredded
- ¼ cup chunky salsa
- A pinch of black pepper

**Directions:**

1. In a bowl, combine the eggs with the water, cheese, salsa and pepper and whisk well.
2. Heat up a pan with the oil over medium-high heat, add the eggs mix, spread into the pan, cook for 3 minutes, flip, cook for 3 more minutes, divide between plates and serve for breakfast.

Enjoy!

**Nutrition:** calories 221, fat 4, fiber 4, carbs 13, protein 7

# Easy Omelet Waffles

**Preparation time:** 10 minutes

**Cooking time:** 5 minutes

**Servings:** 2

**Ingredients:**

- 4 eggs
- A pinch of black pepper
- 2 tablespoons ham, chopped
- ¼ cup low-fat cheddar, shredded
- 2 tablespoons parsley, chopped
- Cooking spray

**Directions:**

1. In a bowl, combine the eggs with pepper, ham, cheese and parsley and whisk really well.
2. Grease your waffle iron with cooking spray, add the eggs mix, cook for 4-5 minutes, divide the waffles between plates and serve them for breakfast.

Enjoy!

**Nutrition:** calories 211, fat 3, fiber 6, carbs 14, protein 8

# Jared Omelets

**Preparation time:** 10 minutes
**Cooking time:** 6 minutes
**Servings:** 2

**Ingredients:**

- Cooking spray
- 2/3 cup low-fat cheddar, shredded
- 4 eggs
- ½ yellow onion, chopped
- ½ cup ham, chopped
- 1 red bell pepper, chopped
- A pinch of black pepper
- 1 tablespoon chives, chopped

## Directions:

1. In a bowl, combine the eggs with onion, ham, bell pepper and pepper and whisk well.
2. Grease 2 mason jars with cooking spray, divide the eggs mix, introduce in the oven and bake at 350 degrees F for 6 minutes.
3. Sprinkle the cheese all over and serve for breakfast.

Enjoy!

**Nutrition:** calories 221, fat 3, fiber 3, carbs 14, protein 7

# Mushrooms And Cheese Omelet

**Preparation time:** 10 minutes

**Cooking time:** 15 minutes

**Servings:** 4

## Ingredients:

- 2 tablespoons olive oil
- A pinch of black pepper
- 3 ounces mushrooms, sliced
- 1 cup baby spinach, chopped
- 3 eggs, whisked
- 2 tablespoons low-fat cheese, grated
- 1 small avocado, peeled, pitted and cubed
- 1 tablespoons parsley, chopped

## Directions:

1. Heat up a pan with the oil over medium-high heat, add mushrooms, stir, cook them for 5 minutes and transfer to a bowl.

2. Heat up the same pan over medium-high heat, add eggs and black pepper, spread into the pan, cook for 7 minutes and transfer to a plate.
3. Spread mushrooms, spinach, avocado and cheese on half of the omelet, fold the other half over this mix, sprinkle parsley on top and serve.

Enjoy!

**Nutrition:** calories 199, fat 3, fiber 4, carbs 14, protein 6

# Egg White Breakfast Mix

**Preparation time:** 10 minutes

**Cooking time:** 10 minutes

**Servings:** 4

**Ingredients:**

- 1 yellow onion, chopped
- 3 plum tomatoes, chopped
- 10 ounces spinach, chopped
- A pinch of black pepper
- 2 tablespoons water
- 12 egg whites
- Cooking spray

## Directions:

1. In a bowl, combine the egg whites with water and pepper and whisk well.
2. Grease a pan with cooking spray, heat up over medium heat, add ¼ of the egg whites, spread into the pan and cook for 2 minutes.
3. Spoon ¼ of the spinach, tomatoes and onion, fold and add to a plate.
4. Repeat with the rest of the egg whites and veggies and serve for breakfast.

Enjoy!

**Nutrition:** calories 235, fat 4, fiber 7, carbs 14, protein 7

# Pesto Omelet

**Preparation time:** 10 minutes
**Cooking time:** 6 minutes
**Servings:** 2

**Ingredients:**

- 2 teaspoons olive oil
- A handful cherry tomatoes, chopped
- 3 tablespoons pistachio pesto
- A pinch of black pepper
- 4 eggs

**Directions:**

1. In a bowl, combine the eggs with cherry tomatoes, black pepper and pistachio pesto and whisk well.
2. Heat up a pan with the oil over medium-high heat, add eggs mix, spread into the pan, cook for 3 minutes, flip, cook for 3 minutes more, divide between 2 plates and serve for breakfast.

Enjoy!

**Nutrition:** calories 199, fat 2, fiber 4, carbs 14, protein 7

# Quinoa Bowls

**Preparation time:** 10 minutes

**Cooking time:** 20 minutes

**Servings:** 2

**Ingredients:**

- 1 peach, sliced
- 1/3 cup quinoa, rinsed
- 2/3 cup low-fat milk
- ½ teaspoon vanilla extract
- 2 teaspoons brown sugar
- 12 raspberries
- 14 blueberries

**Directions:**

1. In a small pan, combine the quinoa with the milk, sugar and vanilla, stir, bring to a simmer over medium heat, cover the pan, cook for 20 minutes and flip with a fork.
2. Divide this mix into 2 bowls, top each with raspberries and blueberries and serve for breakfast.

Enjoy!

**Nutrition:** calories 177, fat 2, fiber 4, carbs 9, protein 8

# Strawberry Sandwich

**Preparation time:** 10 minutes

**Cooking time:** 0 minutes

**Servings:** 4

## Ingredients:

- 8 ounces low-fat cream cheese, soft
- 1 tablespoon stevia
- 1 teaspoon lemon zest, grated
- 4 whole wheat English muffins, halved and toasted
- 2 cups strawberries, sliced

## Directions:

1. In your food processor, combine the cream cheese with the stevia and lemon zest and pulse well.
2. Spread 1 tablespoon of this mix on 1 muffin half and top with some of the sliced strawberries.

3. Repeat with the rest of the muffin halves and serve for breakfast.

Enjoy!

**Nutrition:** calories 211, fat 3, fiber 4, carbs 8, protein 4

# Apple Quinoa Muffins

**Preparation time:** 10 minutes

**Cooking time:** 35 minutes

**Servings:** 4

**Ingredients:**

- ½ cup natural, unsweetened applesauce
- 1 cup banana, peeled and mashed
- 1 cup quinoa
- 2 and ½ cups old-fashioned oats
- ½ cup almond milk
- 2 tablespoons stevia
- 1 teaspoon vanilla extract
- 1 cup water
- Cooking spray
- 1 teaspoon cinnamon powder
- 1 apple, cored, peeled and chopped

**Directions:**

1. Put the water in a small pan, bring to a simmer over medium heat, add quinoa, cook for 15 minutes, fluff with a fork and transfer to a bowl.
2. Add banana, applesauce, oats, almond milk, stevia, vanilla, cinnamon and apple, stir, divide into a muffin pan greases with cooking spray, introduce in the oven and bake at 375 degrees F for 20 minutes.
3. Serve for breakfast.

Enjoy!

**Nutrition:** calories 200, fat 3, fiber 4, carbs 14, protein 7

# Amazing Quinoa Hash Browns

**Preparation time:** 10 minutes

**Cooking time:** 25 minutes

**Servings:** 2

**Ingredients:**

- 1/3 cup quinoa
- 2/3 cup water
- 1 and ½ cups potato, peeled and grated
- 1 eggs
- A pinch of black pepper
- 1 tablespoon olive oil
- 2 green onions, chopped

## Directions:

1. Put the water in a small pan, bring to a simmer over medium heat, add quinoa, stir, cover, cook for 15 minutes and fluff with a fork.
2. IN a bowl, combine the quinoa with potato, egg, green onions and pepper and stir well.
3. Heat up a pan with the oil over medium-high heat, add quinoa hash browns, cook for 5 minutes on each side, divide between 2 plates and serve for breakfast.

Enjoy!

**Nutrition:** calories 191, fat 3, fiber 8, carbs 14, protein 7

# Quinoa Breakfast Bars

**Preparation time:** 2 hours
**Cooking time:** 0 minutes
**Servings:** 6

**Ingredients:**

- ½ cup fat-free peanut butter
- 2 tablespoons coconut sugar
- 1 teaspoon vanilla extract
- ½ teaspoon cinnamon powder
- 1 cup quinoa flakes
- 1/3 cup coconut, flaked
- 2 tablespoons unsweetened chocolate chips

**Directions:**

1. In a large bowl, combine the peanut butter with sugar, vanilla, cinnamon, quinoa, coconut and chocolate chips, stir well, spread on the bottom of a lined baking sheet, press well, cut

in 6 bars, keep in the fridge for 2 hours, divide between plates and serve.

Enjoy!

**Nutrition:** calories 182, fat 4, fiber 4, carbs 13, protein 11

# Quinoa Quiche

**Preparation time:** 10 minutes

**Cooking time:** 45 minutes

**Servings:** 4

**Ingredients:**

- 1` cup quinoa, cooked
- 3 ounces spinach, chopped
- 1 cup fat-free ricotta cheese
- 3 eggs
- 1 and ½ teaspoons garlic powder
- 2/3 cup low-fat parmesan, grated

**Directions:**

1. In a bowl, combine the quinoa with the spinach, ricotta, eggs, garlic powder and parmesan, whisk well, pour into a lined pie pan, introduce in the oven and bake at 355 degrees F for 45 minutes.

2. Cool the quiche down, slice and serve for breakfast.

Enjoy!

**Nutrition:** calories 201, fat 2, fiber 4, carbs 12, protein 7

# Breakfast Quinoa Cakes

**Preparation time:** 10 minutes

**Cooking time:** 30 minutes

**Servings:** 4

**Ingredients:**

- 1 cup quinoa
- 2 cups cauliflower, chopped
- 1 and ½ cups chicken stock
- ½ cup low-fat cheddar, shredded
- ½ cup low-fat parmesan, grated
- 1 egg
- A pinch of black pepper
- 2 tablespoons canola oil

**Directions:**

1. In a pot, combine the quinoa with the cauliflower, stock and pepper, stir, bring to a simmer over medium heat and cook for 20 minutes/
2. Add cheddar and the eggs, stir well, shape medium cakes out of this mix and dredge them in the parmesan.
3. Heat up a pan with the oil over medium-high heat, add the quinoa cakes. cook for 4-5 minutes on each side, divide between plates and serve for breakfast.

Enjoy!

**Nutrition:** calories 199, fat 3, fiber 4, carbs 8, carbs 14, protein 6

# Easy Quinoa Pancakes

**Preparation time:** 10 minutes

**Cooking time:** 6 minutes

**Servings:** 8

## Ingredients:

- ½ cup unsweetened applesauce
- 2 tablespoons coconut sugar
- ½ cup nonfat milk
- 1 tablespoon lemon juice
- 1 teaspoon baking soda
- 1 and ½ cups quinoa flour

## Directions:

1. In your food processor, combine the applesauce with the sugar, milk, lemon juice, baking soda and quinoa and pulse well.
2. Heat up a pan over medium heat, spoon some of the pancake batter, spread into the pan, cook

for 3 minutes on each side and transfer to a plate.
3. Repeat with the rest of the pancake batter, divide the pancakes between plates and serve for breakfast.

Enjoy!

**Nutrition:** calories 188, fat 3, fiber 6, carbs 13, protein 6

# Quinoa And Egg Muffins

**Preparation time:** 10 minutes

**Cooking time:** 30 minutes

**Servings:** 3

**Ingredients:**

- 1/3 cup quinoa, cooked
- 1 zucchini, chopped
- 2 eggs
- 4 egg whites
- ½ cup low-fat feta cheese, shredded
- A pinch of black pepper
- A splash of hot sauce
- Cooking spray

## Directions:

1. In a bowl, combine the quinoa with the zucchini, eggs, egg whites, cheese, black pepper and hot sauce, whisk well and divide into 6 muffin cups greased with the cooking spray.
2. Bake the muffins in the oven at 350 degrees F for 30 minutes.
3. Divide the muffins between plates and serve for breakfast.

Enjoy!

**Nutrition:** calories 221, fat 7, fiber 2, carbs 13, protein 14

# Apple And Quinoa Breakfast Bake

**Preparation time:** 10 minutes

**Cooking time:** 10 minutes

**Servings:** 6

**Ingredients:**

- 1 cup quinoa, cooked
- ¼ teaspoon olive oil
- 2 teaspoons coconut sugar
- 2 apples, cored, peeled and chopped
- 1 teaspoon cinnamon powder
- ½ cup almond milk

**Directions:**

1. Grease a ramekin with the oil, add quinoa, apples, sugar, cinnamon and almond milk, stir, introduce in the oven, bake at 350 degrees F for 10 minutes, divide into bowls and serve.

Enjoy!

**Nutrition:** calories 199, fat 2, fiber 7, carbs 14, protein 8

# Quinoa Patties

**Preparation time:** 10 minutes

**Cooking time:** 20 minutes

**Servings:** 6

**Ingredients:**

- 2 and ½ cups quinoa, cooked
- A pinch of black pepper
- 4 eggs, whisked
- 1 yellow onion, chopped
- ¼ cup chives, chopped
- 1/3 cup low-fat parmesan, grated
- 3 garlic cloves, minced
- 1 cup whole wheat bread crumbs
- 1 tablespoon olive oil

**Directions:**

1.  In a large bowl, combine the quinoa with black pepper, eggs, onion, chives, parmesan, garlic and bread crumbs, stir well and shape medium patties out of this mix.
2.  Heat up a pan with the oil over medium-high heat, add quinoa patties, cook them for 10 minutes on each side, divide them between plates and serve for breakfast.

Enjoy!

**Nutrition:** calories 201, fat 3, fiber 4, carbs 14, protein 8

# Peanut Butter Smoothie

**Preparation time:** 10 minutes
**Cooking time:** 0 minutes
**Servings:** 2

**Ingredients:**

- 2 tablespoons peanut butter
- 2 cups non-fat milk
- 2 bananas, peeled and chopped

**Directions:**

1. In your blender, combine the peanut butter with the milk and bananas, pulse well, divide into 2 glasses and serve.

Enjoy!

**Nutrition:** calories176, fat 4, fiber 6, carbs 14, protein 7

# Yogurt Peanut Butter Mix

**Preparation time:** 10 minutes

**Cooking time:** 0 minutes

**Servings:** 3

**Ingredients:**

- 6 ounces nonfat yogurt
- 2 tablespoons red grapes, halved
- 4 teaspoons grape jelly
- 1 tablespoon fat-free peanut butter
- 1 teaspoons peanuts, chopped

**Directions:**

1. In a bowl, combine the yogurt with the grapes, grape jelly, peanut butter and peanuts, toss well, divide into small cups and serve for breakfast.

Enjoy!

**Nutrition:** calories 187, fat 2, fiber 3, carbs 6, protein 8

# Slow Cooked Oatmeal

**Preparation time:** 10 minutes
**Cooking time:** 8 hours
**Servings:** 3

## Ingredients:

- 4 cups nonfat milk
- 2 cups steel cut pats
- 4 cups water
- 1/3 cup raisins
- 1/3 cup cherries, dried
- 1/3 cup apricots, dried and chopped
- 1 teaspoon cinnamon powder

## Directions:

1. In your slow cooker, combine the milk with the oats, water, raisins, cherries, apricots and cinnamon, stir, cover, cook on Low for 8 hours, divide into bowls and serve for breakfast.

Enjoy!

**Nutrition:** calories 171, fat 3, fiber 6, carbs 15, protein 7

# Salmon Breakfast Salad

**Preparation time:** 10 minutes

**Cooking time:** 0 minutes

**Servings:** 2

**Ingredients:**

- 3 tablespoons nonfat yogurt
- 1 teaspoon horseradish sauce
- 1 tablespoon dill, chopped
- 1 teaspoon lemon juice
- 4 ounces smoked salmon, boneless, skinless and torn
- 3 ounces salad greens
- 2 ounces cherry tomatoes, halved
- 2 ounces black olives, pitted and sliced

**Directions:**

1. In a salad bowl, combine the salmon with salad greens, tomatoes and black olives.

2. In another bowl, combine the yogurt with horseradish, dill and lemon juice, whisk well, pour over the salad, toss well and serve for breakfast.

Enjoy!

**Nutrition:** calories 177, fat 4, fiber 7, carbs 14, protein 8

# Banana And Pear Breakfast Salad

**Preparation time:** 10 minutes

**Cooking time:** 0 minutes

**Servings:** 2

**Ingredients:**

- 1 banana, peeled and sliced
- 1 Asian pear, cored and cubed
- Juice of ½ lime
- ½ teaspoon cinnamon powder
- 2 ounces pepitas, toasted

**Directions:**

1. In a bowl, combine the banana with the pear, lime juice, cinnamon and pepitas, toss, divide between small plates and serve for breakfast.

Enjoy!

**Nutrition:** calories 188, fat 2, fiber 3, carbs 5, protein 7

# Simple Plum And Avocado Salad

**Preparation time:** 10 minutes

**Cooking time:** 0 minutes

**Servings:** 3

**Ingredients:**

- 2 avocados, peeled, pitted and cubed
- 4 plums, stones removed and cubed
- 1 cup cilantro, chopped
- 1 garlic clove, minced
- Juice of 1 lemon
- A drizzle of olive oil
- 1 red chili pepper, minced

**Directions:**

1. In a salad bowl, combine the avocados with plums, cilantro, garlic, lemon juice, oil and chili pepper, toss well, divide between plates and serve for breakfast.

Enjoy!

**Nutrition:** calories 212, fat 2, fiber 4, carbs 14, protein 11

# Cherries Oatmeal

**Preparation time:** 10 minutes

**Cooking time:** 15 minutes

**Servings:** 6

**Ingredients:**

- 2 cups old-fashioned oats
- 6 cups water
- 1 cup almond milk
- 1 teaspoon cinnamon powder
- 1 teaspoon vanilla extract
- 2 cups cherries, pitted and sliced

## Directions:

1. In a small pot, combine the oats with the water, milk, cinnamon, vanilla and cherries, toss, bring to a simmer over medium-high heat, cook for 15 minutes, divide into bowls and serve for breakfast.

Enjoy!

**Nutrition:** calories 180, fat 4, fiber 4, carbs 9, protein 7

# Orange And Apricots Oatmeal

**Preparation time:** 10 minutes

**Cooking time:** 15 minutes

**Servings:** 4

**Ingredients:**

- 1 and ½ cups water
- 1 cup steel cut oats
- 1 cup orange juice
- 2 tablespoons apricots, dried and chopped
- 2 tablespoons coconut sugar
- 2 tablespoons pecans, chopped
- ¼ teaspoon cinnamon powder

**Directions:**

1. In a small pot, combine the oats with the water, orange juice, apricots, sugar, cinnamon and pecans, stir, bring to a simmer over medium heat, cook for 15 minutes, divide into bowls and serve for breakfast.

Enjoy!

**Nutrition:** calories 190, fat 3, fiber 6, carbs 8, protein 5

# Cinnamon Pear Oatmeal

**Preparation time:** 10 minutes
**Cooking time:** 15 minutes
**Servings:** 3

**Ingredients:**

- 3 cups water
- 1 cup steel cut oats
- 1 tablespoon cinnamon powder
- 1 cup pear, cored, peeled and cubed

**Directions:**

1. In a small pot, combine the water with the oats, cinnamon and pear, toss, bring to a simmer over medium heat, cook for 15 minutes, divide into bowls and serve for breakfast.

Enjoy!

**Nutrition:** calories 171, fat 2, fiber 5, carbs 11, protein 6

# Banana And Walnuts Bowls

**Preparation time:** 10 minutes

**Cooking time:** 15 minutes

**Servings:** 4

**Ingredients:**

- 2 cups water
- 1 cup steel cut oats
- 1 cup almond milk
- ¼ cup walnuts, chopped
- 2 tablespoons chia seeds
- 2 bananas, peeled and mashed
- 1 teaspoon vanilla extract

**Directions:**

1. In a small pot, combine the water with the oats, milk, walnuts, chia seeds, bananas and vanilla, toss, bring to a simmer over medium

heat, cook for 15 minutes, divide into bowls and serve for breakfast.

Enjoy!

**Nutrition:** calories 162, fat 4, fiber 6, carbs 11, protein 4

# Parsley Omelet

**Preparation time:** 10 minutes

**Cooking time:** 6 minutes

**Servings:** 6

**Ingredients:**

- 2 tablespoons almond milk
- A pinch of black pepper
- 6 eggs, whisked
- 2 tablespoons parsley, chopped
- 1 tablespoon low-fat cheddar cheese, shredded
- 2 teaspoons olive oil

**Directions:**

1. In a bowl, mix the eggs with the milk, black pepper, parsley and cheese and whisk well.
2. Heat up a pan with the oil over medium-high heat, add the eggs mix, spread into the pan, cook for 3 minutes, flip, cook for 3 minutes more, divide between plates and serve for breakfast.

Enjoy!

**Nutrition:** calories 200, fat 4, fiber 6, carb 13, protein 9

# Cheddar Baked Eggs

**Preparation time:** 10 minutes

**Cooking time:** 15 minutes

**Servings:** 4

## Ingredients:

- 4 eggs
- 4 slices low-fat cheddar
- 2 spring onions, chopped
- 1 tablespoon olive oil
- A pinch of black pepper
- 1 tablespoon cilantro, chopped

## Directions:

1. Grease 4 ramekins with the oil, sprinkle green onions in each, crack an egg in each ramekins and top with cilantro and cheddar cheese.
2. Introduce in the oven and bake at 375 degrees F for 15 minutes.

3. Serve for breakfast.

Enjoy!

**Nutrition:** calories 199, fat 3, fiber 7, carbs 11, protein 5

# Hash Brown Mix

**Preparation time:** 10 minutes
**Cooking time:** 30 minutes
**Servings:** 6

**Ingredients:**

- Cooking spray
- 6 eggs
- 2 cups hash browns
- ¼ cup non-fat milk
- ½ cup fat-free cheddar cheese, shredded
- 1 small yellow onion, chopped
- A pinch of black pepper
- ½ green bell pepper, chopped
- ½ red bell pepper, chopped

**Directions:**

1. Heat up a pan greased with cooking spray over medium-high heat, add onions, green

and red bell pepper, stir and cook for 4-5 minutes.

2. Add hash browns and black pepper, stir and cook for 5 minutes more.
3. In a bowl, combine the eggs with milk and cheese, whisk well, pour over the mix from the pan, introduce in the oven and bake at 380 degrees F for 20 minutes.
4. Slice, divide between plates and serve.

Enjoy!

**Nutrition:** calories 221, fat 4, fiber 5, carbs 14, protein 6

# Peaches Mix

**Preparation time:** 10 minutes
**Cooking time:** 5 minutes
**Servings:** 4

**Ingredients:**

- 6 small peaches, cored and cut into wedges
- ¼ cup coconut sugar
- 2 tablespoons non-fat butter
- ¼ teaspoon almond extract

**Directions:**

1. In a small pan, combine the peaches with sugar, butter and almond extract, toss, cook over medium-high heat for 5 minutes, divide into bowls and serve for breakfast.

Enjoy!

**Nutrition:** calories 198, fat 2, fiber 6, carbs 11, protein 8

# Cinnamon Brown Rice Pudding

**Preparation time:** 10 minutes

**Cooking time:** 25 minutes

**Servings:** 4

**Ingredients:**

- 1 cup brown rice
- 1 and ½ cups water
- 1 tablespoon vanilla extract
- 1 tablespoon cinnamon powder
- 1 tablespoon non-fat butter
- ½ cup coconut cream, unsweetened

**Directions:**

1. In a pot, combine the rice with the water, vanilla, cinnamon, butter and cream, stir, bring to a simmer over medium heat, cook for 25 minutes, divide into bowls and serve for breakfast.

Enjoy!

**Nutrition:** calories 182, fat 4, fiber 7, carbs 11, protein 6

# BOOK 2

# FRESH
# SUMMER
# RECIPES FOR

# LUNCH

# LIGHT AND HEALTHY LUNCH

# Beef Lunch Bowls

**Preparation time:** 10 minutes

**Cooking time:** 20 minutes

**Servings:** 6

**Ingredients:**

- 8 ounces beef sirloin steak, trimmed, fat removed and cut into cubes
- ½ cup red onion, chopped
- ¼ cup tomatoes, chopped
- ¾ cup fat-free cheddar, grated
- 2 tablespoons low-fat sour cream
- 7 tablespoons salsa
- 1 tablespoon olive oil
- 2 tablespoons cilantro, chopped

**Directions:**

1. Heat up a pan with the oil over medium-high heat, add the steak cubes, stir and brown them for 4 minutes on each side.

2. Add onion, tomatoes and cream,, toss, cover, cook for 10 minutes more, divide into bowls, sprinkle cheese, salsa and cilantro on top and serve.

Enjoy!

**Nutrition:** calories 251, fat 4, fiber 7, carbs 16, protein 7

# Creamy Chicken Breast

**Preparation time:** 10 minutes

**Cooking time:** 20 minutes

**Servings:** 4

**Ingredients:**

- 1 tablespoon olive oil
- A pinch of black pepper
- 2 pounds chicken breasts, skinless, boneless and cubed
- 4 garlic cloves, minced
- 2 and ½ cups low-sodium chicken stock
- 2 cups coconut cream
- ½ cup low-fat parmesan, grated
- 1 tablespoon basil, chopped

## Directions:

1. Heat up a pan with the oil over medium-high heat add chicken cubes and brown them for 3 minutes on each side.
2. Add garlic, black pepper, stock and cream, toss, cover the pan and cook everything for 10 minutes more.
3. Add cheese and basil, toss, divide between plates and serve for lunch.

Enjoy!

**Nutrition:** calories 221, fat 6, fiber 9, carbs 14, protein 7

# Indian Chicken Stew

**Preparation time:** 1 hour

**Cooking time:** 20 minutes

**Servings:** 4

**Ingredients:**

- 1 pound chicken breasts, skinless, boneless and cubed
- 1 tablespoon garam masala
- 1 cup fat-free yogurt
- 1 tablespoon lemon juice
- A pinch of black pepper
- ¼ teaspoon ginger, ground
- 15 ounces tomato sauce, no-salt-added
- 5 garlic cloves, minced
- ½ teaspoon sweet paprika

**Directions:**

1. In a bowl, mix the chicken with garam masala, yogurt, lemon juice, black pepper and ginger,

toss well, cover and leave in the fridge for 1 hour.

2. Heat up a pan over medium heat, add chicken mix, toss and cook for 5-6 minutes.
3. Add tomato sauce, garlic and paprika, toss, cook for 15 minutes, divide between plates and serve for lunch.

Enjoy!

**Nutrition:** calories 221, fat 6, fiber 9, carbs 14, protein 16

# Chicken, Bamboo And Chestnuts Mix

**Preparation time:** 10 minutes

**Cooking time:** 20 minutes

**Servings:** 4

**Ingredients:**

- 1 pound chicken thighs, boneless, skinless and cut into medium chunks
- 1 cup low-sodium chicken stock
- 1 tablespoon olive oil
- 2 tablespoons coconut aminos
- 1-inch ginger, grated
- 1 carrot, sliced
- 2 garlic cloves, minced
- 8 ounces canned bamboo shoots, no-salt-added and drained
- 8 ounces water chestnuts

**Directions:**

1. Heat up a pan with the oil over medium-high heat, add chicken, stir and brown for 4 minutes on each side
2. Add the stock, aminos, ginger, carrot, garlic, bamboo and chestnuts, toss, cover the pan and cook everything over medium heat for 12 minutes.
3. Divide everything between plates and serve.

Enjoy!

**Nutrition:** calories 281, fat 7, fiber 9, carbs 14, protein 14

# Chuck Roast And Veggies

**Preparation time:** 10 minutes

**Cooking time:** 1 hour and 30 minutes

**Servings:** 6

**Ingredients:**

- 4 pounds lean chuck roast, fat removed
- 2 yellow onions, roughly chopped
- 1 cup low-sodium beef stock
- 1 tablespoon thyme, chopped
- 2 celery sticks, chopped
- 2 carrots, sliced
- 3 garlic cloves, minced
- A pinch of black pepper

**Directions:**

1. In a roasting pan, combine the roast with the onions, stock, thyme, celery, carrots, garlic and a pinch of pepper, introduce in the oven and

roast at 400 degrees F for 1 hour and 30 minutes.

2. Slice the roast, divide it and the veggies from the pot between plates and serve for lunch. Enjoy!

**Nutrition:** calories 321, fat 7, fiber 11, carbs 14, protein 11

# Salsa Chicken

**Preparation time:** 10 minutes

**Cooking time:** 25 minutes

**Servings:** 4

**Ingredients:**

- 1 cup mild salsa, no-salt-added
- ½ teaspoon cumin, ground
- Black pepper to the taste
- 1 tablespoon chipotle paste
- 1 pound chicken thighs, skinless and boneless
- 2 cups corn
- Juice of 1 lime
- ½ tablespoon olive oil
- 2 tablespoons cilantro, chopped
- 1 cup cherry tomatoes, halved
- 1 small avocado, pitted, peeled and cubed

## Directions:

1. In a pot, combine the salsa with the cumin, black pepper, chipotle paste, chicken thighs and corn, toss, bring to a simmer and cook over medium heat for 25 minutes.
2. Add lime juice, oil, cherry tomatoes and avocado, toss, divide into bowls and serve for lunch.

Enjoy!

**Nutrition:** calories 269, fat 6, fiber 9, carbs 18, protein 7

# Tomato Soup

**Preparation time:** 10 minutes

**Cooking time:** 20 minutes

**Servings:** 4

**Ingredients:**

- 3 garlic cloves, minced
- 1 yellow onion, chopped
- 3 carrots, chopped
- 15 ounces tomato sauce, no-salt-added
- 1 tablespoon olive oil
- 15 ounces roasted tomatoes, no-salt-added
- 1 cup low-sodium veggie stock
- 1 tablespoon tomato paste, no-salt-added
- 1 tablespoon basil, dried
- ¼ teaspoon oregano, dried
- 3 ounces coconut cream
- A pinch of black pepper

**Directions:**

1. Heat up a pot with the oil over medium heat, add garlic and onion, stir and cook for 5 minutes.
2. Add carrots, tomato sauce, tomatoes, stock, tomato paste, basil, oregano and black pepper, stir, bring to a simmer, cook for 15 minutes, add cream, blend the soup using an immersion blender, divide into bowls and serve for lunch.

Enjoy!

**Nutrition:** calories 261, fat 6, fiber 9, carbs 15, protein 7

# Easy Pork Chops

**Preparation time:** 10 minutes

**Cooking time:** 20 minutes

**Servings:** 4

**Ingredients:**

- 4 pork chops, boneless
- 1 tablespoon olive oil
- 1 cup chicken stock, low-sodium
- A pinch of black pepper
- 1 teaspoon sweet paprika

**Directions:**

1. Heat up a pan with the oil over medium-high heat, add pork chops, brown them for 5 minutes on each side, add paprika, black pepper and stock, toss, cook for 15 minutes more, divide between plates and serve with a side salad.

Enjoy!

**Nutrition:** calories 272, fat 4, fiber 8, carbs 14, protein 17

# Cod Soup

**Preparation time:** 10 minutes

**Cooking time:** 25 minutes

**Servings:** 4

**Ingredients:**

- 1 yellow onion, chopped
- 12 cups low-sodium fish stock
- 1 pound carrots, sliced
- 1 tablespoon olive oil
- Black pepper to the taste
- 2 tablespoons ginger, minced
- 1 cup water
- 1 pound cod, skinless, boneless and cut into medium chunks

**Directions:**

1. Heat up a pot with the oil over medium-high heat, add onion, stir and cook for 4 minutes.

2. Add water, stock, ginger and carrots, stir and cook for 10 minutes more.
3. Blend soup using an immersion blender, add the fish and pepper, stir, cook for 10 minutes more, ladle into bowls and serve.

Enjoy!

**Nutrition:** calories 261, fat 6, fiber 2, carbs 11, protein 9

# Easy Beef Stew

**Preparation time:** 10 minutes

**Cooking time:** 1 hour and 20 minutes

**Servings:** 6

**Ingredients:**

- 2 and ½ pounds beef brisket, fat removed
- 2 bay leaves
- 4 cups low-sodium beef stock
- 4 carrots, chopped
- 3 garlic cloves, chopped
- 1 green cabbage head, shredded
- Black pepper to the taste

**Directions:**

1. Put the beef brisket in a pot, add stock, pepper, garlic and bay leaves, bring to a simmer over medium heat and cook for 1 hour.
2. Add carrots and cabbage, stir, cook for 30 minutes more, divide into bowls and serve for lunch.

Enjoy!

**Nutrition:** calories 271, fat 8, fiber 3, carbs 16, protein 9

# Sweet Potato Soup

**Preparation time:** 10 minutes

**Cooking time:** 1 hour and 40 minutes

**Servings:** 6

**Ingredients:**

- 4 big sweet potatoes
- 28 ounces veggie stock
- A pinch of black pepper
- ¼ teaspoon nutmeg, ground
- 1/3 cup low-sodium heavy cream

**Directions:**

1. Arrange the sweet potatoes on a lined baking sheet, bake them at 350 degrees F for 1 hour and 30 minutes, cool them down, peel, roughly chop them and put them in a pot.
2. Add stock, nutmeg, cream and pepper, pulse really well using an immersion blender, heat

the soup over medium heat, cook for 10 minutes, ladle into bowls and serve. Enjoy!

**Nutrition:** calories 235, fat 4, fiber 5, carbs 16, protein 8

# Sweet Potatoes And Zucchini Soup

**Preparation time:** 10 minutes

**Cooking time:** 20 minutes

**Servings:** 8

## Ingredients:

- 4 cups veggie stock
- 2 tablespoons olive oil
- 2 sweet potatoes, peeled and cubed
- 8 zucchinis, chopped
- 2 yellow onions, chopped
- 1 cup coconut milk
- A pinch of black pepper
- 1 tablespoon coconut aminos
- 4 tablespoons dill, chopped
- ½ teaspoon basil, chopped

**Directions:**

1. Heat up a pot with the oil over medium heat, add onion, stir and cook for 5 minutes.
2. Add zucchinis, stock, basil, potato and pepper, stir and cook for 15 minutes more.
3. Add milk, aminos and dill, pulse using an immersion blender, ladle into bowls and serve for lunch.

Enjoy!

**Nutrition:** calories 283, fat 3, fiber 4, carbs 14, protein 9

# Lemongrass And Chicken Soup

**Preparation time:** 10 minutes

**Cooking time:** 25 minutes

**Servings:** 4

**Ingredients:**

- 4 lime leaves, torn
- 4 cups veggie stock, low-sodium
- 1 lemongrass stalk, chopped
- 1 tablespoon ginger, grated
- 1 pound chicken breast, skinless, boneless and cubed
- 8 ounces mushrooms, chopped
- 4 Thai chilies, chopped
- 13 ounces coconut milk
- ¼ cup lime juice
- ¼ cup cilantro, chopped
- A pinch of black pepper

**Directions:**

1. Put stock into a pot, bring to a simmer over medium heat, add lemongrass, ginger and lime leaves, stir, cook for 10 minutes, strain into another pot and heat up again over medium heat again.
2. Add chicken, mushrooms, milk, cilantro, black pepper, chilies and lime juice, stir, simmer for 15 minutes, ladle into bowls and serve.

Enjoy!

**Nutrition:** calories 150, fat 4, fiber 4, carbs 6, protein 7

# Easy Lunch Salmon Steaks

**Preparation time:** 10 minutes

**Cooking time:** 20 minutes

**Servings:** 4

**Ingredients:**

- 1 big salmon fillet, cut into 4 steaks
- 3 garlic cloves, minced
- 1 yellow onion, chopped
- Black pepper to the taste
- 2 tablespoons olive oil
- ¼ cup parsley, chopped
- Juice of 1 lemon
- 1 tablespoon thyme, chopped
- 4 cups water

**Directions:**

1. Heat up a pan with the oil over medium-high heat, add onion and garlic, stir and cook for 3 minutes.

2. Add black pepper, parsley, thyme, water and
   lemon juice, stir, bring to a gentle boil, add
   salmon steaks, cook them for 15 minutes,
   drain, divide between plates and serve with a
   side salad for lunch.

Enjoy!

**Nutrition:** calories 203, fat 3, fiber 6, carbs 8, protein 10

# Simple Summer Beef Salad

**Preparation time:** 10 minutes

**Cooking time:** 16 minutes

**Servings:** 4

**Ingredients:**

- 2 tomatoes, chopped
- 2 avocados, pitted and chopped
- 6 cups lettuce leaves, chopped
- 1 small red onion, chopped
- 1 tablespoon olive oil
- 1 teaspoon chili powder
- Juice of 2 limes
- 1 yellow onion, chopped
- 1 pound beef, ground
- 2 garlic cloves, minced
- 1 teaspoon cumin, ground
- Black pepper to the taste
- 1 bunch cilantro, chopped

## Directions:

1. Heat up a pan with the oil over medium-high heat, add the yellow onion, stir and cook for 5 minutes.
2. Add garlic, pepper, cumin and chili powder, stir and cook for 1 minute.
3. Add beef, stir and cook for 10 minutes and take off heat.
4. In a salad bowl, mix lettuce with avocados, tomatoes, red onion and cilantro and stir.
5. Add beef mix and lime juice, toss to coat and serve for lunch.

Enjoy!

**Nutrition:** calories 143, fat 6, fiber 4, carbs 12, protein 6

# Sausage Skillet

**Preparation time:** 10 minutes

**Cooking time:** 13 minutes

**Servings:** 2

**Ingredients:**

- 1 pound sausage, sliced
- ½ red bell pepper, chopped
- 1 yellow onion, chopped
- 1 bunch kale, chopped
- 1 tomato, chopped
- Black pepper to the taste

**Directions:**

1. Heat up a pan over medium-high heat, add sausage, stir and brown on all sides for 3 minutes.
2. Add onions, tomato, bell pepper, black pepper and kale, stir, cook for 10 minutes, divide between plates and serve.

Enjoy!

**Nutrition:** calories 220, fat 3, fiber 4, carbs 11, protein 9

# Light Balsamic Salad

**Preparation time:** 10 minutes

**Cooking time:** 0 minutes

**Servings:** 3

**Ingredients:**

- 1 orange, cut into segments
- 2 green onions, chopped
- 1 romaine lettuce head, torn
- 1 avocado, pitted, peeled and cubed
- ¼ cup almonds, sliced

*For the salad dressing:*

- 1 teaspoon mustard
- ¼ cup olive oil
- 2 tablespoons balsamic vinegar
- Juice of ½ orange
- Salt and black pepper

**Directions:**

1. In a salad bowl, mix oranges with avocado, lettuce, almonds and green onions.
2. In another bowl, mix olive oil with vinegar, mustard, orange juice, salt and pepper, whisk well, add this to your salad, toss and serve.

Enjoy!

**Nutrition:** calories 120, fat 2, fiber 2, carbs 4, protein 8

# Cauliflower Soup

**Preparation time:** 10 minutes

**Cooking time:** 50 minutes

**Servings:** 4

**Ingredients:**

- 3 pounds cauliflower, florets separated
- 1 yellow onion, chopped
- 1 tablespoon coconut oil
- Black pepper to the taste
- 2 garlic cloves, minced
- 2 carrots, chopped
- 2 cups beef stock
- 1 cup water
- ½ cup coconut milk
- 1 teaspoon olive oil
- 2 tablespoons parsley, chopped

## Directions:

1. Heat up a pot with the coconut oil over medium-high heat, add carrots, onion and garlic, stir and cook for 5 minutes.
2. Add cauliflower, water and stock, stir, bring to a boil, cover and cook for 45 minutes.
3. Transfer soup to your blender and pulse well, add coconut milk, pulse well again, ladle into bowls, drizzle the olive oil over the soup, sprinkle parsley and serve for lunch.

Enjoy!

**Nutrition:** calories 190, fat 2, fiber 1, carbs 16, protein 4

# Purple Potato Soup

**Preparation time:** 10 minutes

**Cooking time:** 1 hour and 15 minutes

**Servings:** 6

**Ingredients:**

- 6 purple potatoes, chopped
- 1 cauliflower head, florets separated
- Black pepper to the taste
- 4 garlic cloves, minced
- 1 yellow onion, chopped
- 3 tablespoons olive oil
- 1 tablespoon thyme, chopped
- 1 leek, chopped
- 2 shallots, chopped
- 4 cups chicken stock, low-sodium

## Directions:

1. In a baking dish, mix potatoes with onion, cauliflower, garlic, pepper, thyme and half of the oil, toss to coat, introduce in the oven and bake for 45 minutes at 400 degrees F.
2. Heat up a pot with the rest of the oil over medium-high heat, add leeks and shallots, stir and cook for 10 minutes.
3. Add roasted veggies and stock, stir, bring to a boil, cook for 20 minutes, transfer soup to your food processor, blend well, divide into bowls and serve.

Enjoy!

**Nutrition:** calories 200, fat 8, fiber 6, carbs 15, protein 8

# Broccoli Soup

**Preparation time:** 10 minutes

**Cooking time:** 1 hour

**Servings:** 4

**Ingredients:**

- 2 pounds broccoli, florets separated
- 1 yellow onion, chopped
- 1 tablespoon olive oil
- Black pepper to the taste
- 1 cup celery, chopped
- 2 carrots, chopped
- 3 and ½ cups low-sodium chicken stock
- 1 tablespoon cilantro chopped

## Directions:

1. Heat up a pot with the oil over medium-high heat, add the onion, celery and carrots, stir and cook for 5 minutes.
2. Add broccoli, black pepper and stock, stir and cook over medium heat for 1 hour.
3. Pulse using an immersion blender, add cilantro, stir the soup again, divide into bowls and serve.

Enjoy!

**Nutrition:** calories 170, fat 2, fiber 1, carbs 10, protein 9

# Leeks Soup

**Preparation time:** 10 minutes

**Cooking time:** 1 hour and 15 minutes

**Servings:** 6

## Ingredients:

- 2 gold potatoes, chopped
- 1 cup cauliflower florets
- Black pepper to the taste
- 5 leeks, chopped
- 4 garlic cloves, minced
- 1 yellow onion, chopped
- 3 tablespoons olive oil
- A handful parsley, chopped
- 4 cups low-sodium chicken stock

## Directions:

1. Heat up a pot with the oil over medium-high heat, add onion and garlic, stir and cook for 5 minutes.

2.  Add potatoes, cauliflower, black pepper, leeks and stock, stir, bring to a simmer, cook over medium heat for 30 minutes, blend using an immersion blender, add parsley, stir, ladle into bowls and serve.

Enjoy!

**Nutrition:** calories 150, fat 8, fiber 6, carbs 7, protein 8

# Cauliflower Lunch Salad

**Preparation time:** 2 hours
**Cooking time:** 10 minutes
**Servings:** 4

**Ingredients:**

- 1/3 cup low-sodium veggie stock
- 2 tablespoons olive oil
- 6 cups cauliflower florets, grated
- Black pepper to the taste
- ¼ cup red onion, chopped
- 1 red bell pepper, chopped
- Juice of ½ lemon
- ½ cup kalamata olives, pitted and cut into halves
- 1 teaspoon mint, chopped
- 1 tablespoon cilantro, chopped

## Directions:

1. Heat up a pan with the oil over medium-high heat, add cauliflower, pepper and stock, stir, cook for 10 minutes, transfer to a bowl and keep in the fridge for 2 hours.
2. Mix cauliflower with olives, onion, bell pepper, black pepper, mint, cilantro and lemon juice, toss to coat and serve.

Enjoy!

**Nutrition:** calories 185, fat 12, fiber 6, carbs 11, protein 8

# Shrimp Soup

**Preparation time:** 10 minutes

**Cooking time:** 15 minutes

**Servings:** 6

### Ingredients:

- 46 ounces low-sodium chicken stock
- 3 cups shrimp, peeled and deveined
- A pinch of black pepper
- 2 tablespoons green onions, chopped
- 1 teaspoon dill, chopped

### Directions:

1. Put the stock in a pot, bring to a simmer over medium heat, add black pepper, onion and shrimp, stir and simmer for 8-10 minutes.
2. Add dill, stir, cook for 5 minutes more, ladle into bowls and serve.

Enjoy!

**Nutrition:** calories 190, fat 7, fiber 2, carbs 12, protein 8

# Shrimp Mix

**Preparation time:** 10 minutes
**Cooking time:** 10 minutes
**Servings:** 4

**Ingredients:**

- 1 and ½ pounds shrimp, peeled and deveined
- 1 tablespoon olive oil
- 1 teaspoon sesame seeds
- 24 ounces broccoli florets
- 1 green onion, chopped
- 1 tablespoon balsamic vinegar
- 2 garlic cloves, minced
- 1 tablespoon ginger, grated

**Directions:**

1. In a bowl, mix oil with vinegar, garlic and ginger and whisk.
2. Transfer this to a pan, heat up over medium heat, add shrimp, stir and cook for 3 minutes.
3. Add broccoli, stir, cook for 4 minutes more,
4. Add sesame seeds and green onions, toss, divide everything between plates and serve.

Enjoy!

**Nutrition:** calories 265, fat 2, fiber 1, carbs 10, protein 20

# Green Beans Stew

**Preparation time:** 10 minutes

**Cooking time:** 25 minutes

**Servings:** 4

**Ingredients:**

- 2 tablespoons olive oil
- 2 carrots, chopped
- 1 yellow onion, chopped
- 20 ounces green beans
- 2 garlic cloves, minced
- 7 ounces canned tomatoes, chopped
- 5 cups low-sodium veggie stock
- A pinch of black pepper
- 1 tablespoon parsley, chopped

**Directions:**

1. Heat up a pot with the oil, over medium heat, add onion, stir and cook for 5 minutes.

2. Add carrots, green beans, garlic, tomatoes, black pepper and stock, stir, cover and simmer over medium heat for 20 minutes.
3. Add parsley, divide into bowls and serve for lunch.

Enjoy!

**Nutrition:** calories 281, fat 5, fiber 1, carbs 14, protein 11

# Mushroom And Veggie Soup

**Preparation time:** 10 minutes

**Cooking time:** 25 minutes

**Servings:** 4

**Ingredients:**

- 1 yellow onion, chopped
- A pinch of black pepper
- 1 tablespoon olive oil
- 1 red chili pepper, chopped
- 2 carrots, sliced
- 4 garlic cloves, minced
- 12 mushrooms, chopped
- 2 ounces kale leaves, roughly chopped
- 4 cups low-sodium veggie stock
- 1 cup tomatoes, chopped
- ½ tablespoon lemon zest, grated
- ½ tablespoon parsley, chopped

**Directions:**

1. Heat up a pot with the oil, over medium heat, add onion, garlic, chili and carrots, stir and sauté for 5 minutes.
2. Add black pepper, mushrooms, kale, tomatoes, stock and lemon zest, stir, cover and cook over medium heat for 20 minutes.
3. Add parsley, toss, divide into bowls and serve for lunch.

Enjoy!

**Nutrition:** calories 200, fat 6, fiber 6, carbs 9, protein 10

# Jackfruit And Chili Stew

**Preparation time:** 10 minutes

**Cooking time:** 25 minutes

**Servings:** 4

**Ingredients:**

- 40 ounces canned jackfruit
- 14 ounces canned red chili puree
- 1 yellow onion, chopped
- 8 garlic cloves, minced
- 1 tablespoon olive oil
- 6 cups low-sodium veggie stock
- 1 tablespoon oregano, chopped
- 1 tablespoon cilantro, chopped

**Directions:**

1. Heat up a pot with the oil, over medium-high heat, add onion and garlic, stir and cook for 4-5 minutes.
2. Add jackfruit, chili puree and stock, stir, cover and cook over medium heat for 15 minutes.
3. Add oregano and cilantro, stir, cook for 5 minutes more, divide into bowls and serve.

Enjoy!

**Nutrition:** calories 263, fat 6, fiber 7, carbs 13, protein 11

# Chickpeas Stew

**Preparation time:** 10 minutes

**Cooking time:** 40 minutes

**Servings:** 4

**Ingredients:**

- 1 teaspoon olive oil
- 1 cup chickpeas, soaked for 8 hours and drained
- 4 garlic cloves, minced
- 1 yellow onion, chopped
- 1 green chili pepper, chopped
- 1 teaspoon coriander, ground
- ½ teaspoon cumin, ground
- ½ teaspoon sweet paprika
- 2 tomatoes, chopped
- 1 and ½ cups low-sodium veggie stock
- A pinch of black pepper
- 3 cups spinach leaves
- 1 tablespoon lemon juice

## Directions:

1. Heat up a pot with the oil over medium heat, add garlic, onion and chili pepper, stir and cook for 5 minutes.
2. Add coriander, cumin, paprika and black pepper, stir and cook for 5 minutes more.
3. Add chickpeas, tomatoes, stock and lemon juice, stir, cover the pot, cook over medium heat for 25 minutes, add spinach, cook for 5 minutes more, divide into bowls and serve.

Enjoy!

**Nutrition:** calories 270, fat 7, fiber 6, carbs 14, protein 9

# Eggplant Stew

**Preparation time:** 10 minutes

**Cooking time:** 20 minutes

**Servings:** 4

**Ingredients:**

- ½ teaspoon cumin seeds
- 1 tablespoon coriander seeds
- ½ teaspoon mustard seeds
- 1 tablespoon olive oil
- 1 tablespoon ginger, grated
- 2 garlic cloves, minced
- 1 green chili pepper, chopped
- A pinch of cinnamon powder
- ½ teaspoon cardamom, ground
- ½ teaspoon turmeric powder
- 1 teaspoon lime juice
- 4 baby eggplants, cubed
- 1 cup low-sodium veggie stock
- 1 tablespoon cilantro, chopped

**Directions:**

1. Heat up a pot with the oil over medium-high heat, add cumin, coriander and mustard seeds, stir and cook them for 5 minutes.
2. Add ginger, garlic, chili, cinnamon, cardamom and turmeric, stir and cook for 5 minutes more.
3. Add lime juice, eggplants and stock, stir, cover and cook over medium heat for 15 minutes.
4. Add cilantro, stir, divide into bowls and serve for lunch.

Enjoy!

**Nutrition:** calories 270, fat 4, fiber 6, carbs 12, protein 9

# Delicious Veggie Quesadillas

**Preparation time:** 10 minutes

**Cooking time:** 4 minutes

**Servings:** 3

**Ingredients:**

- 1 cup black beans, cooked
- ½ red bell pepper, chopped
- 4 tablespoons cilantro, chopped
- ½ cup corn
- 1 cup low-fat cheddar, shredded
- 6 whole wheat tortillas
- 1 carrot, shredded
- 1 small jalapeno pepper, chopped
- 1 cup non-fat yogurt
- Juice of ½ lime

**Directions:**

1. Divide black beans, red bell pepper, 2 tablespoons cilantro, corn, carrot, jalapeno and the cheese on half of the tortillas and cover with the other ones.
2. Heat up a pan over medium-high heat, add one quesadilla, cook for 3 minutes on one side, flip, cook for 1 more minute on the other and transfer to a plate.
3. Repeat with the rest of the quesadillas.
4. In a bowl, combine 2 tablespoons cilantro with yogurt and lime juice, whisk well and serve next to the quesadillas.

Enjoy!

**Nutrition:** calories 200, fat 3, fiber 4, carbs 13, protein 7

# Chicken Wraps

**Preparation time:** 10 minutes

**Cooking time:** 10 minutes

**Servings:** 4

**Ingredients:**

- 8 ounces chicken breast, cubed
- ½ cup celery, chopped
- 2/3 cup mandarin oranges, chopped
- ¼ cup onion, chopped
- A drizzle of olive oil
- 2 tablespoons mayonnaise
- ¼ teaspoon garlic powder
- A pinch of black pepper
- 4 whole wheat tortillas
- 4 lettuce leaves

**Directions:**

1. Heat up a pan with the oil over medium-high heat, add chicken cubes, cook for 5 minutes on each side and transfer to a bowl.
2. Divide the chicken on each tortilla, also divide celery, oranges, onion, mayo, garlic powder, black pepper and lettuce leaves, wrap and serve for lunch.

Enjoy!

**Nutrition:** calories 200, fat 3, fiber 4, carbs 13, protein 7

# Black Bean Patties

**Preparation time:** 10 minutes

**Cooking time:** 10 minutes

**Servings:** 4

**Ingredients:**

- 2 whole wheat bread slices, torn
- 3 tablespoons cilantro, chopped
- 2 garlic cloves, minced
- 15 ounces canned black beans, no-salt-added, drained and rinsed
- 6 ounces canned chipotle peppers, chopped
- 1 teaspoon cumin, ground
- 1 egg
- Cooking spray
- ½ avocado, peeled, pitted and mashed
- 1 tablespoon lime juice
- 1 cherry tomato, chopped

## Directions:

1. Put the bread in your food processor, pulse well and transfer bread crumbs to a bowl.
2. Combine them with cilantro, garlic, black beans, chipotle peppers, cumin and egg, stir well and shape 4 patties out of this mix.
3. Heat up a pan over medium-high heat, grease with cooking spray, add beans patties, cook them for 5 minutes on each side and transfer to plates.
4. In a bowl, combine the avocado with tomato and lime juice, stir well, add over the patties and serve for lunch.

Enjoy!

**Nutrition:** calories 200, fat 4, fiber 4, carbs 12, protein 8

# Lunch Rice Bowls

**Preparation time:** 10 minutes

**Cooking time:** 5 minutes

**Servings:** 2

**Ingredients:**

- 1 teaspoon olive oil
- 1 cup mixed bell peppers, onion, zucchini and corn, chopped
- 1 cup chicken meat, cooked and shredded
- 1 cup brown rice, cooked
- 3 tablespoons salsa
- 2 tablespoons low-fat cheddar, shredded
- 2 tablespoons low-fat sour cream

**Directions:**

1. Heat up a pan with the oil over medium-high heat, add mixed veggies, stir and cook them for 5 minutes.
2. Divide the rice and the chicken meat into 2 bowls, add mixed veggies and top each with salsa, cheese and sour cream.
3. Serve for lunch.

Enjoy!

**Nutrition:** calories 199, fat 4, fiber 4, carbs 12, protein 7

# Lunch Salmon Salad

**Preparation time:** 10 minutes

**Cooking time:** 0 minutes

**Servings:** 3

**Ingredients:**

- 1 cup canned salmon, flaked
- 1 tablespoon lemon juice
- 3 tablespoons fat-free yogurt
- 2 tablespoons red bell pepper, chopped
- 1 teaspoon capers, drained and chopped
- 1 tablespoon red onion, chopped
- 1 teaspoon dill, chopped
- A pinch of black pepper
- 3 whole wheat bread slices

**Directions:**

1. In a bowl, combine the salmon with the lemon juice, yogurt, bell pepper, capers, onion, dill and black pepper and stir well.

2. Spread this on each bread slice and serve for lunch.

Enjoy!

**Nutrition:** calories 199, fat 2, fiber 4, carbs 14, protein 8

# Stuffed Mushrooms Caps

**Preparation time:** 10 minutes

**Cooking time:** 15 minutes

**Servings:** 2

**Ingredients:**

- 2 Portobello mushroom caps
- 2 tablespoons pesto
- 2 tomato, chopped
- ¼ cup low-fat mozzarella, shredded

**Directions:**

1. Divide pesto, tomato and mozzarella in each mushroom cap, arrange them on a lined baking sheet, introduce in the oven and bake at 400 degrees F for 15 minutes.
2. Serve for lunch.

Enjoy!

**Nutrition:** calories 198, fat 3, fiber 4, carbs 14, protein 9

# Lunch Tuna Salad

**Preparation time:** 10 minutes
**Cooking time:** 0 minutes
**Servings:** 3

**Ingredients:**

- 5 ounces canned tuna in water, drained
- 1 tablespoon red vinegar
- 1 tablespoon olive oil
- ¼ cup green onions, chopped
- 2 cups arugula
- 1 tablespoon low-fat parmesan, grated
- A pinch of black pepper
- 2 ounces whole wheat pasta, cooked

**Directions:**

1. In a bowl, combine the tuna with the vinegar, oil, green onions, arugula, pasta and black pepper and toss.
2. Divide between 3 plates, sprinkle parmesan on top and serve for lunch.

Enjoy!

**Nutrition:** calories 200, fat 4, fiber 4, carbs 14, protein 7

# Shrimp Lunch Rolls

**Preparation time:** 10 minutes
**Cooking time:** 0 minutes
**Servings:** 4

### Ingredients:

- 12 rice paper sheets, soaked for a few seconds in warm water and drained
- 1 cup cilantro, chopped
- 12 basil leaves
- 12 baby lettuce leaves
- 1 small cucumber, sliced
- 1 cup carrots, shredded
- 20 ounces shrimp, cooked, peeled and deveined

### Directions:

1. Arrange all rice papers on a working surface, divide cilantro, bay leaves, baby lettuce leaves,

cucumber, carrots and shrimp, wrap, seal edges and serve for lunch.

Enjoy!

**Nutrition:** calories 200, fat 4, fiber 4, carbs 14, protein 8

# Veggie Soup

**Preparation time:** 10 minutes

**Cooking time:** 16 minutes

**Servings:** 6

**Ingredients:**

- 2 teaspoons olive oil
- 1 and ½ cups carrot, shredded
- 6 garlic cloves, minced
- 1 cup yellow onion, chopped
- 1 cup celery, chopped
- 32 ounces low-sodium chicken stock
- 4 cups water
- 1 and ½ cups whole wheat pasta
- 2 tablespoons parsley, chopped
- ¼ cup low-fat parmesan, grated

## Directions:

1. Heat up a pot with the oil over medium-high heat, add garlic, stir and cook for 1 minute.
2. Add onion, carrot and celery, stir and cook for 7 minutes.
3. Add stock, water and pasta, stir, bring to a boil over medium heat and cook for 8 minutes more.
4. Divide into bowls, top each with parsley and parmesan and serve.

Enjoy!

**Nutrition:** calories 212, fat 4, fiber 4, carbs 13, protein 8

# Melon And Avocado Lunch Salad

**Preparation time:** 10 minutes

**Cooking time:** 0 minutes

**Servings:** 4

**Ingredients:**

- 2 tablespoons stevia
- 2 tablespoon red vinegar
- 2 tablespoons mint, chopped
- A pinch of black pepper
- 1 avocado, peeled, pitted and sliced
- 4 cups baby spinach
- ½ small cantaloupe, peeled and cubed
- 1 and ½ cups strawberries, sliced
- 2 teaspoons sesame seeds, toasted

**Directions:**

1. In a salad bowl, combine the avocado with baby spinach, cantaloupe and strawberries and toss.
2. In another bowl, combine the stevia with vinegar, mint and black pepper, whisk, add to your salad, toss, sprinkle sesame seeds on top and serve.

Enjoy!

**Nutrition:** calories 199, fat 3, fiber 4, carbs 12, protein 8

# Spaghetti Squash And Sauce

**Preparation time:** 10 minutes

**Cooking time:** 25 minutes

**Servings:** 4

**Ingredients:**

- 1 pound beef, ground
- ½ cup yellow onion, chopped
- ½ cup green bell pepper, chopped
- 2 garlic cloves, minced
- 14 ounces canned tomatoes, no-salt-added, chopped
- 2 tablespoons tomato paste
- 8 ounces tomato sauce
- 1 teaspoon Italian seasoning
- ¼ cup low-fat parmesan, shredded
- 2 pounds spaghetti squash, pricked with a knife

## Directions:

1. Put the spaghetti squash on a lined baking sheet, introduce in the oven, bake at 400 degrees F for 10 minutes, cut into halves, shred and separate squash pulp into spaghetti and put into a bowl.
2. Heat up a pan over medium-high heat, add the beef, stir and brown for 5 minutes.
3. Add onion, bell pepper, garlic, tomatoes, tomato paste, tomato sauce and Italian seasoning, stir and cook for 10 minutes.
4. Divide the squash spaghetti between plates, top each with beef mix, sprinkle parmesan on top and serve.

Enjoy!

**Nutrition:** calories 231, fat 4, fiber 5, carbs 14, protein 9

# Sausage And Potatoes Mix

**Preparation time:** 10 minutes

**Cooking time:** 22 minutes

**Servings:** 6

**Ingredients:**

- ½ pound smoked sausage, cooked and chopped
- 3 tablespoons olive oil
- 1 and ¾ pounds red potatoes, cubed
- 2 yellow onions, chopped
- 1 teaspoon thyme, dried
- 2 teaspoons cumin, ground
- A pinch of black pepper

**Directions:**

1. Heat up a pan with the oil over medium-high heat, add potatoes and onions, stir and cook for 12 minutes.

2. Add sausage, thyme, cumin and black pepper, stir, cook for 10 minutes more, divide between plates and serve for lunch.

Enjoy!

**Nutrition:** calories 199, fat 2, fiber 4, carbs 14, protein 8

# Beef Soup

**Preparation time:** 10 minutes

**Cooking time:** 20 minutes

**Servings:** 4

**Ingredients:**

- 1 tablespoon olive oil
- 1 yellow onion, chopped
- 1 pound beef sirloin, ground
- 32 ounces low-sodium beef stock
- 1/3 cup whole wheat flour
- 1 pound mixed carrots and celery, chopped

**Directions:**

1. Heat up a pot with the oil over medium-high heat, add beef and flour, stir well and brown for 5 minutes.
2. Add onion, carrots, celery and stock, stir, bring to a simmer, reduce heat to medium, cook the

soup for 15 minutes, ladle into bowls and serve for lunch.

Enjoy!

**Nutrition:** calories 281, fat 3, fiber 5, carbs 14, protein 11

# Lunch Shrimp Salad

**Preparation time:** 10 minutes
**Cooking time:** 8 minutes
**Servings:** 4

**Ingredients:**

- 12 ounces asparagus spears, trimmed and halved
- 8 ounces baby corn
- 12 endive leaves, torn
- 12 baby lettuce leaves
- 12 spinach leaves
- 12 ounces shrimp, cooked, peeled and deveined
- 2 and ½ cups red raspberries
- ¼ cup olive oil
- ¼ cup raspberry vinegar
- 1 tablespoon cilantro, chopped
- 2 teaspoons stevia

## Directions:

1. Put some water in a pot, bring to a boil over medium-high heat, add asparagus, cook for 8 minutes, transfer to a bowl filled with ice water, cool down, drain well and put in a salad bowl.
2. Add corn, endive leaves, spinach, lettuce, shrimp and raspberries.
3. In another bowl, combine the oil with the vinegar, stevia and cilantro, whisk well, add to your salad, toss and serve for lunch.

Enjoy!

**Nutrition:** calories 199, fat 2, fiber 3, carbs 14, protein 8

# Watercress, Asparagus And Shrimp Salad

**Preparation time:** 10 minutes

**Cooking time:** 4 minutes

**Servings:** 4

## Ingredients:

- 12 ounces asparagus spears, trimmed
- 16 ounces shrimp, cooked, peeled and deveined
- 4 cups watercress, torn
- 2 cups cherry tomatoes, halved
- ¼ cup raspberry vinegar
- ¼ cup olive oil

## Directions:

1. Put the asparagus in a pot, add water to cover, cook over medium heat for 4 minutes, drain, transfer to a bowl filled with ice water, cool down, drain again and transfer to a salad bowl.

2.  Add shrimp, watercress, tomatoes, raspberry vinegar and oil, toss well and serve for lunch. Enjoy!

**Nutrition:** calories 212, fat 4, fiber 7, carbs 14, protein 9

# Lunch Chicken Tacos

**Preparation time:** 10 minutes
**Cooking time:** 0 minutes
**Servings:** 2

**Ingredients:**

- 4 mini taco shells
- 2 tablespoons celery, chopped
- 1 tablespoon light mayonnaise
- 1 tablespoon salsa
- 1 tablespoon low-fat cheddar, shredded
- 1/3 cup chicken, cooked and shredded

**Directions:**

1. In a bowl, combine the celery with the mayo, salsa, cheddar and chicken and toss well.
2. Spoon this into mini taco shells and serve for lunch.

Enjoy!

**Nutrition:** calories 221, fat 3, fiber 8, carbs 14, protein 9

# Millet Cakes

**Preparation time:** 10 minutes

**Cooking time:** 55 minutes

**Servings:** 4

**Ingredients:**

- 1 tablespoon olive oil
- 1 cup millet
- ¼ cup yellow onion, chopped
- 1 garlic clove, minced
- 3 and ½ cups water
- A pinch of black pepper
- 1/3 cup zucchini, shredded
- 1/3 cup carrot, shredded
- 1/3 cup low-fat parmesan, grated
- 1 and ½ teaspoon thyme, chopped
- 1 teaspoon lemon zest, grated
- Cooking spray

## Directions:

1. Heat up a pan with 1 tablespoon olive oil over medium heat, add onion, stir and cook for 4 minutes.
2. Add garlic and millet, stir and cook for 1 more minute.
3. Add the water and a pinch of black pepper, stir, cover, reduce heat to low and cook for 20 minutes stirring once.
4. Add carrot, zucchini, thyme, parmesan and lemon zest, stir and cook for 10 minutes more.
5. Leave the millet mix to cool down, shape 12 millet cakes using damp hands and put them on a working surface.
6. Heat up a pan with cooking spray over medium-high heat, add millet cakes, cook them for 5 minutes on each side, divide them between plates and serve.

Enjoy!

**Nutrition:** calories 211, fat 4, fiber 4, carbs 14, protein 6

# Lentils Dal

**Preparation time:** 10 minutes

**Cooking time:** 10 minutes

**Servings:** 4

**Ingredients:**

- 1 and ½ teaspoons olive oil
- 1 yellow onion, chopped
- 2 teaspoons curry powder
- 14 ounces canned lentils, no-salt-added, drained and rinsed
- 14 ounces canned tomatoes, chopped
- 2 pounds chicken, roasted, and chopped
- A pinch of black pepper
- ¼ cup low-fat yogurt

**Directions:**

1. Heat up a pot with the oil over medium-high heat, add onion, stir and brown for 4 minutes.

2. Add curry powder, stir and cook for 1 more minute.

3. Add lentils, tomatoes, chicken and black pepper, stir, cook for 5 minutes more, take off heat, add the yogurt, toss, divide into bowls and serve for lunch.

Enjoy!

**Nutrition:** calories 199, fat 3, fiber 7, carbs 17, protein 8

# Italian Pasta Mix

**Preparation time:** 10 minutes

**Cooking time:** 20 minutes

**Servings:** 4

**Ingredients:**

- 1 pound whole wheat penne pasta, cooked
- 3 garlic cloves, minced
- 2 tablespoons olive oil
- 3 carrots, sliced
- 1 bunch asparagus, trimmed and cut into medium pieces
- 1 red bell pepper, chopped
- 1 yellow bell pepper, chopped
- 1 cup cherry tomatoes, halved
- A pinch of black pepper
- 2/3 cup coconut cream
- 2 tablespoons low-fat parmesan, grated

**Directions:**

1. Heat up a pan with the oil over medium-high heat, add the garlic, stir and cook for 2 minutes.
2. Add carrots, stir and cook for 4 minutes more.
3. Add asparagus, stir, cover the pan and cook for 8 minutes more.
4. Add yellow and red bell peppers, stir and cook for 5 minutes.
5. Add cherry tomatoes, black pepper, cream, parmesan and pasta, toss, divide between plates and serve.

Enjoy!

**Nutrition:** calories 221, fat 4, fiber 4, carbs 15, protein 9

# Glazed Ribs

**Preparation time:** 10 minutes

**Cooking time:** 1 hour and 20 minutes

**Servings:** 4

**Ingredients:**

- 1 rack pork ribs, ribs separated
- 1 and ¼ cups tomato sauce
- ¼ cup white vinegar
- 3 tablespoons spicy mustard
- 2 tablespoons coconut sugar
- 3 tablespoons water
- ¼ teaspoon hot sauce
- 1 teaspoon onion powder
- Cooking spray

**Directions:**

1. Put the ribs in a baking dish, cover with tin foil and bake in the oven at 400 degrees F for 1 hour.

2. Heat up a pan with the tomato sauce, mustard, sugar, vinegar, water, onion powder and hot sauce, stir, cook for 10 minutes and take off heat.
3. Baste the ribs with half of this sauce, place them on preheated grill over medium-high heat, grease them with cooking spray, cook for 4 minutes on each side, divide between plates and serve with the rest of the sauce on the side.

Enjoy!

**Nutrition:** calories 287, fat 5, fiber 8, carbs 16, protein 15

# Pork Chops And Sauce

**Preparation time:** 10 minutes

**Cooking time:** 9 hours

**Servings:** 6

**Ingredients:**

- 6 pork loin chops
- 1 tablespoon olive oil
- 2 tablespoons tapioca, crushed
- 1 yellow onion, chopped
- 10 ounces low-sodium cream of mushroom soup
- ½ cup apple juice
- 2 teaspoons thyme, chopped
- 1 and ½ cups mushrooms, sliced
- ¼ teaspoon garlic powder

**Directions:**

1. Heat up a pan with the oil over medium-high heat, add pork chops, brown them for 4

minutes on each side and transfer to a slow cooker.

2. Add crushed tapioca, onion, cream of mushroom soup, apple juice, thyme, mushrooms and garlic powder, toss, cover and cook on Low for 9 hours.
3. Divide the pork chops and sauce between plates and serve.

Enjoy!

**Nutrition:** calories 229, fat 4, fiber 9, carbs 16, protein 17

# Shrimp And Pomegranate Sauce

**Preparation time:** 10 minutes

**Cooking time:** 50 minutes

**Servings:** 4

**Ingredients:**

- 1-quart pomegranate juice
- ½ cup coconut sugar
- ¼ cup lemon juice
- 1 pound shrimp, peeled and deveined
- ½ teaspoon cumin, ground
- ¾ teaspoon coriander, ground
- ¼ teaspoon cinnamon powder
- 1 and ½ tablespoons olive oil
- A pinch of black pepper
- 4 cups baby arugula

**Directions:**

1. In a pan, combine the pomegranate juice with lemon juice and sugar, stir, bring to a simmer over medium heat and cook for 45 minutes.
2. In a bowl, combine the shrimp with the cumin, cinnamon, coriander, black pepper and the oil and toss well.
3. Heat up a pan over medium heat, add shrimp, cook for 2 minutes on each side and transfer to a bowl.
4. Add arugula and the pomegranate sauce, toss and serve for lunch.

Enjoy!

**Nutrition:** calories 281, fat 5, fiber 8, carbs 17, protein 14

# THANK YOU

Thank you for choosing *Complete Summer Cookbook 2021* for improving your cooking skills! I hope you enjoyed making the recipes as much as tasting them! If you're interested in learning new recipes and new meals to cook, go and check out the other books of the series.

CPSIA information can be obtained
at www.ICGtesting.com
Printed in the USA
BVHW091522020621
608633BV00002B/125